Story•Medicine, By Sez Kristiansen

STORY•MEDICINE

Written by Sez Kristiansen

Copyright © Sez Kristiansen

Cover art by Sez Kristiansen

All rights reserved.

No part of this publication may be reproduced, distributed, or transmitted in any forms or by any means, including photography, recording, or other electronic, or mechanical methods, without the prior written permission of the publisher, except in the case of brief quotations embodied in critical reviews and certain other non-commercial uses permitted by copyright law.

hello@sezkristiansen.com

www.sezkristiansen.com

≈

Other books, kindle editions & audiobooks by Sez Kristiansen:

Inspired Mama *(non-fiction guide for free-spirited mothers)*

Healing HER *(poetry for healing through feminine energy)*

Story Medicine *(poetry & prose for every soul-sickness)*

The Daily Heal Journal *(guided prompt companion)*

The Spoken Remedy *(podcast of meditations & poetry)*

≈

This book

is dedicated to those

who seek a remedy

of which *this* world

cannot heal alone.

TABLE•OF•CONTENTS

INTRODUCTION	8
THE•EXHALE	14
THE•CONVERSATION	16
THE•FALL	19
THE•FIX	22
THE•EXILE	23
THE•OCEAN•WOMAN	25
THE•LESSER•HARDSHIP	28
THE•LIMINALITY	30
THE•PASSION	33
THE•TRUTH	35
THE•GARDENER	37
THE•LIFEBOATS	41
THE•WINTER•BEE	43
THE•BREATH•AND•THE•WATER	45
THE•FUTURE	48
THE•FRIEND	51
THE•UNDOING	54
THE•FALCON	56

THE•BODY•OF•WATER	60
THE•WILDER•KNOWING	61
THE•FALSE•SUN	63
THE•BELONGING	64
THE•QUESTION	66
THE•WISDOM•OF	67
•UNWANTEDNESS	67
THE•FALSEHOOD	69
THE•REPLENISHED	71
THE•CHILD	72
THE•REWILDING	73
THE•REMAKING	76
THE•DREAMER	78
THE•EXPOSED•ROOT	81
THE•GIVER	84
THE•MOUNTAIN	86
THE•BELOVED	88
THE•LANDSCAPE	90
THE•RECIEVER	94
THE•REAL•LOSS	97
THE•LATTICE	98

THE•REBIRTH	100
THE•MAGICK	102
THE•NATURE•WITHIN	105
THE•VISION	107
THE•TRANSMISSION	109
THE•BAREFOOT	110
THE•TRUER•LOVE	111
THE•INVERTION	112
THE•POTTER	114
THE•QUIET•PLACE	115
THE•WOLF•AND•THE•ARROW	117
THE•REMEDY	121
THE•WILD, DEAR•CHILD	122
THE•HOPE	124
THE•SOVEREIGNTY	126
THE•END	129

INTRODUCTION

You are a prolific storyteller.

You can ink and edit your life at will, depending on your emotional dictionary. And even in your silence, blank pages unfurl in your wake. And even in your dreams, your pages keep turning. And even as you hold your breath, a finger stalls on the ellipsis of your inhale with anticipation...

Your storybook's spine and your own are one, and your entire life exists between the definitive bookends of birth and death.

Here you are right now, somewhere in the middle of your book as the storyteller, the lead character and the very book itself. The content of your autobiography depends very much upon those whose stories you carry with you - and which ones you tend to believe in.

We all carry the weight of other people's stories. They are the faint dents imprinted onto our clean pages from past narratives. They have created furrowed lines for us to follow suit and any form of free writing or spontaneity requires a very brave and steady hand. If you are familiar with the struggle of living the same story over and over again, if you have come to intimately know the paradox of being both the creat*or* and what is being creat*ed* - then you will have come to understand that repetition is truly the death of art. And what is this life if not the energy of some greater creator expressing itself through you?

Have you ever felt a deep desire to look up from the page of your current life to see what exists outside of this limiting narrative? When you can no longer bear your own story, when you feel like you have been engraved with a prophecy that isn't yours to fulfill…when you want to contain more poetry than a birth certificate and a eulogy; there is remedy in the form of *symbolic language*.

Symbolic language is a form of poetry, verse and short story that echoes deep from within your being. As an empath, creative and highly sensitive being, you are particularly attuned to this form of remedy because you already hold the power of emotion which allows you to cross a threshold between the two worlds. Emotions are gifts given from the unseen to help you make sense of what *is* seen. They act like living bridges that carry you across from the earthly - to the Divine. And they are a native language in themself.

Ancient traditions have known the combined power of emotion, nature and story for centuries. They harnessed it through song, myth, fairytale, folklore, archetype and poetry; administering a specific story to a patient whose imbalances could not be understood by the mind alone. Something much more potent was needed for the one who suffered from deep beneath the human bone.

This is still deeply distressing state felt in our collective today but it has been normalized due to the absence of our local story-bearer. These emotional, psychological and spiritual imbalances are now labeled in the dictionary as depression, grief, disease, and anxiety, and are medicated in ways that splinter us further from not only embodying our deeper wholeness but from connecting to the cyclical nature of life that keeps us in conversation with The Great Mystery.

Story is not an object or an artifact but a living being that helps us make sense of the ineffable. Without symbolic language how could we possibly begin to describe what is most mysterious and Divine in this world? How could we begin to articulate *love* most authentically without art, dance or song? How could we dare to rebirth ourselves without following the journey of the warrior archetype? How could the existential be spoken about without our tongues twisting in ethereal ways? Pain would lose its meaning, along with the language we require to heal it.

These days, we live in a type of soul-famine from the story medicine that used to nourish and connect us to the greater order of the cosmos - to our place in the natural world and our purpose in the community. But we still have the ability to self-medicate, and it is equally potent. Reading, listening and creating our own narrative, still laced with the healing qualities of symbolism is our Northern Star as heart-centered beings.

Movement is a healing narrative.
Creativity is a healing narrative.
Dream is a healing narrative.
Nature is a healing narrative.
Silence is a healing narrative.
Love is a healing narrative.

To find remedy in any of the above expressions, just look at how deeply multi-faceted and limitless they are. *Feel* how expressionate they are and how symbolic they are towards our holistic wellness. When you create, spirit speaks. When you move, spirit speaks. When you spend time in intentional silence, spirit most certainly speaks. These are all dialogues that bridge your earthly body with whomever God represents to you.

Long-term emotional imbalances are often caused by our limited, one-dimensional and singular story. This is the type of story that doesn't have the capacity to trust what is felt and not seen. It doesn't entertain character changes (our own and in others). And it certainly does not make space for duality. This one-dimensional story is limited to a bigotry narrative, based on definitive labels that enforce us into a certain kind of conformed helplessness that offers no room for potentiality. But that is what you are; a blank page full of potential and never at any point in your life *just one story*.

Many Native American traditions use the word "medicine" to refer to anything that has spiritual power and that keeps us *walking in beauty*.

Each poem, short story and prose in this book is a remedy to the things that cause us to forget what walking in beauty feels like and empowers us to re-story our limiting and repetitive narrative into multi-dimensional abstracts of art from which we can heal ourselves and our collective through.

These stories have been wildcrafted from the wilderness: the one within and without - the one above and below – the one we live in now and the one our ancestors call us back to through the eaves. They seam the two worlds together to make medicine for deep and restorative healing.

It is said that *there is a story remedy for every soul-sickness you experience in your life. All you have to do is find it.* I hope this book offers you the remedial seeds of symbolic, metaphoric and emotive language, so that you may begin to plant your own medicinal garden within yourself. May you find the remedy you seek and have the courage to share your medicine with the world.

THE•EXHALE

This past year

has been one

prolonged

i n h a l e.

One held in

and forgotten

breath.

One great heave

of bone

and breast.

One fell swoop

that buckled knees

and curdled dreams.

But now -

it's time to let go.

It's time

to learn how

to breathe again.

(It's ok…

the body remembers how.)

THE·CONVERSATION

We all long

to hold a deeper

conversation

with life.

A familiar,

yet inexplicable

longing to

converse with the

elements.

To repair our clothes

with pine needles

and the fibers

of milkweed.

To let our young

run wild under the cosmos,

protected by

shields of wisdom and

the singing blades of grass.

We long to whisper

to the whales

deep below the ice

and hum lullabies with the

soft breeze that cradles

sun's warmth in its cradle.

We long

to participate in

an existence

we often don't feel

part of.

And in that longing

we are made human -

but it's in the following

of that unraveling thread,

that we are weaved back

into our spirits.

So heed the drum's song

that cannot be separated

from that of your heart's skin,

for it beats the song of

your homecoming.

THE•FALL

It's time to

ready the earth,

till the soil,

give some lungs to

the tightly packed ground

laden with years of fallen dreams.

The seeds of past trauma,

of futures ever distant,

still bed down in the damp ground.

Time to unearth

what has been long left

in the dark.

Time to undo a lifetime

of labor that offered

but meager harvest

to hungry soul.

No more heaping on new dreams

to make up for the ones that

were lost to first frost.

It's time to gather

the know-how,

find fortitude and fearlessness.

Time to cull

a life with deeper roots,

riper fruits,

and more potent balms for

tender hearts.

Today we consciously decide

to fall apart and

to face the fray,

knowing we must first

come undone

to see the infinite amount of ways

we can be remade.

THE•FIX

Only when you stop seeking for what will fix you - will you start to heal from what's kept you broken.

Because it's in your search for perfection that you deny the very truth of who you are. You are already: whole, loved, worthy, valued, home...

Feeling broken comes from an illusion of what *wholeness* is supposed to look and feel like.

But wholeness looks messy. It feels like months spent in gutters. It looks like chaos. It feels like sweet iron and damp earth. It looks like years of tear-stained notebooks. It feels like a body full of invisible scars. It looks like a drowning disguised as a wave. It feels like emotional salt-water crocodiles hiding in your belly. It feels like a heart encumbered by thorns - but a willingness to hold it anyway.

It's not our brokenness that needs fixing - but our idea of what's considered *whole* that needs radical amending.

THE·EXILE

It sometimes feels like

the search for 'better and more'

burrows crevasses within us,

just to fill us with flaws

that were not there to begin with,

that were never in question…

but now we feel uncertain,

now we feel destined

to rove in exile

from where we already belong

from what we already have

from what's never been wrong

from who we already are

and what we already know

blinded and guided

by a hunger to grow

what's only just been seeded

and calling for Heart,

our inward attention,

our intentions to start

seeking less from what's out there

and more from our own soil,

what's already planted within us,

and what's always been whole.

THE·OCEAN·WOMAN

Once, not long ago, your spirit sat by the shore between this world and the other. It watched in agony as schools of fish darted in-between vibrant corals and lamented as luminous seaweed rocked back and forth with the tide.

Spirit gazed upon the flickering lights across the bay that seemed to ash up towards the night's starry sky, and sat with a heavy longing to be part of that other world, full of form, flesh and contour. *How can I be made real*, it thought. *How can I come to learn about the art of living when I am neither brush nor paint, neither flesh nor bone, have neither breath nor beat in my body?* And so in its grief, spirit flared itself so courageously through the night that it made itself a lighthouse of longing.

By dawn, the Great Mother had come to spirit's shore and spoke. "I feel your longing, dear spirit. I recognize it as my own to create something from nothing. Come, and we will make matter, so you may travel across to the other world." Spirit could barely express its gratitude before the Great Mother began to lift up her waves, like a tulle skirt full of netted pleats and spindrift hems. She gathered all she could from the depths of her abundant parlor: shells, pebbles, old oak trunks that had been washed away by storms, fine seagrass, soft sand and translucent kelp. The Great Mother spun and shaped, cut and cast, until soon, a human form came into being. She was more beautiful than spirit could have imagined and tossed its long beams of light up towards the morning sky in celebration. The Great Mother brought this bric-a-brac of a woman, this sea-made-maiden, into life by placing a full moon in her belly and then blew salty air into her lungs. Spirit danced with such delight and such joy that the Great Mother wrapped her earthy skin around spirit in warmth and love. As they embraced, the sun birthed over the horizon, spelling a new day into the worlds.

"Listen spirit, and listen well." The Great Mother spoke. "You must take this water woman to the otherworld and bring her life as much joy as you bring me. You must guide her through whatever darkness befalls upon her. Be her courage and her will against all illusions that might lie on the other side of those banks. You must always remind her of her truth and where she comes from. Usher her back into remembrance with an insatiable longing that no other journey can satisfy.

Give yourself to her and she will manifest you into the form you desire through her creativity. Then you will get to live through her art, through her words, through her love and her tears." With their agreement, spirit danced into the body of the ocean woman, where it knew it would reside until eventually, the years of salt would erode the body away and the quiet black tide would come to take her home again.

The Great Mother cast a bridge across the two worlds and placed one last item inside the ocean woman's chest; a beautiful crimson conch, so she would be able to hear the echoes of spirit call from within her. "This heart is your communication, dear spirit, use it to speak to ocean woman in your mother tongue, for the otherworld may not understand that which is subtle and felt. Go now and learn what it is to be of form, but never forget what it is to be without. Use love's echo as your language."

And without hesitation, the ocean woman and spirit danced across the bridge towards the otherworld with a sacred agreement that spirit would be given life - and ocean woman's life would be given to spirit.

THE•LESSER•HARDSHIP

Choose the lesser

hardship…

because escaping your pain

may create more distance than

sitting with it.

And ignoring your longings

may be more neglectful

than following them.

And hushing your heart

may be more deafening

than allowing it to speak.

And keeping it together

may create more wreckage

than falling apart.

And all the fears

you hold in making the right choice,

may be heavier than

the simple acts

that free them.

Invite the escape

the longing

and the fear

not into conversation

but into presence,

with you.

For the greater famine

is in your hunger

for so much to be otherwise.

THE•LIMINALITY

Where do you go from here,

when *here*

is all you have left...

No road revealed itself

so clearly

as the one you

never expected to find

within the wilderness

of your loss.

No hope blossomed

so fiercely

as the one seeded

in life's darkest winter.

No light more

gratefully received

than the one

fracturing from the

lighthouse of your

own heart.

You may not know

what comes next

but your body holds

a harbor for you to

rest within

until time and tide

lifts your little lifeboat

up and out

towards open seas.

For now,

Rest *is* the journey.

Slow *is* the journey.

Surrender *is* the journey.

And when there feels to be no way out –

there is always a way back *in*.

THE·PASSION

Your creative talents

are smoke signals.

Wake up every morning,

ready to tend to their fires,

ready to throw handfuls

of dry green grass

upon last night's ash,

ready to ignite sleepy tinder

with full lungs

and hold damp cloth

over the flames.

Watch these creations burn

and puff out signals

to those who speak your language,

to those who read *soul*

to those who have

walked long to find you

and would lose their way

if you gave up on

your fires.

Let your passion be the flame

that unites your tribe

and offers itself

towards the ignition

of others.

THE·TRUTH

Another's truth

is not yours to own.

And not all truths

are weapons

but buds,

learning to bloom,

learning to seed

themselves

and protect

themselves

and hold

themselves…

Truth is a trellis

one builds around their heart,

so that they may be

surrounded by

that which

offers most

support.

Truth is a flower

one holds so gently

within their palm,

without the need

to weaponize it -

but a deeper need

to nurture it

for one's own beauty.

THE·GARDENER

To sit by the flower bed
and tend
to that which
no longer bears life…
to that which
no longer *gives* life,
but offers its body instead
to the soil
so it may be
of use and nourishment.

That is the
job of the humble gardener.

To cut away
that which no longer
brings harmony to their
tender plot.

That is the task
within your hands.

For you *are* the humble gardener
the giver of life and death
to all that lives within
this flowerbed
of life and of dream.

Yours are the nurturing hands
to which all
is brought to
life through.

The heart to which
all hope must be sung from.
And some days may bring
you to tears
for the despair
that is to know
when something must
die.

But with those tears,
you bathe
what will come
anew.

You moisten the
earth that has
long been parched
of hope.

Such is the gardener's
sacred work:
the knowing
the trusting
and the very act itself.
The gardener's heart

is one covered in dirt
and splayed with flyaway
grass blades.

It is a heart that knows
which part of her garden
is to be
kept wild
and which part needs
a little more direction.

You are the gardener,
and when winter casts it's
heavy veil
making
earth into ice -
it's time to
lay your tools down.

For no betterment can
be made in those dark days.
Only slow and rest
can help nurture
what is to be rebirthed.
Such is the intuitive work
of the one who knows
life and her cycles,
who knows that their
inner life too
follows a cyclical nature

of healing and hope,
but too,
of death and necessary endings.

You are the caretaker
of all that has been given
a place to grow within your heart
and your work
has never been to
empty your energy
into the sickly plant
who's being kept alive
because you cannot bear
its loss.

Turn now, towards
that which offers a future,
to the labor
of love
that will bring forth
this new idea,
this new dream
this new hope.

You are the humble gardener.
May your hard work
create a place where
you may walk
your soul home through.

THE·LIFEB_O_ATS

Hold on tight

to those knees.

Bring them up close

towards chest.

Fasten your arms

around them.

And arc your spine over,

so you are able to

tuck limbs into

the creases and folds

of this body-raft.

These knees

are two small lifeboats,

keeping you buoyant,

holding out the storm

as you rock

back and forth.

Your heart,

a lighthouse, flaring

out into the long night.

You are safe here.

This body, this raft

can contain

the magnitude of your

of your ache.

And there is no shame

in self-refuge.

THE·WINTER·BEE

In winter, honeybees stay within the hive and form a cluster of warmth and self-nourishment. Only the females survive this winter period, (the workers and their queen) while the male drones die away until they are needed again in spring. The female workers shiver and shake their bodies within their cluster, creating a bubble of heat out of small, instinctual movements. The colder the weather, the tighter the cluster. The hive moves through shifts, continually changing those who stand at the cold and vulnerable outer circle with those warmest and closest to the queen. The queen - the creator, the one who holds life and brings it into the world - remains highly protected until the warmer weather returns.

And so it is that this highly organized monarchy survives months and months of severe cold, isolation and hardship. They seem to lack any means of comfort or an environment that allows them to flourish, and yet they are abundant in exactly what is needed to survive.

So too are you gifted with this instinctual ability during the winter of your own life. It is an ability to cut away at the masculine energy within you that demands for action, risk and boldness, and instead, settle into the intuitive and raw energy of the psyche.

It's a time for small movements, ones that protect the life-bearing monarch within you. It's time to form clusters of support that offer a little nourishment and warmth every day.

Like the honeybee in winter, you may not feel like you have what you need to thrive and flourish - but you do possess everything you need within yourself to survive this cycle of hardship.

When the time is right, risk action and boldness will call again. It will be time to bring your creations, ideas and projects to light. It will be a time of outer work and manifestation.

For now, however, make this time slow and sacred, make it intentional and simple – only then can your heart be tended to by a body of workers who know how to hold you.

THE·BREATH·AND·THE·WATER

Take your burdened body to the water;
the bruises, the births,
the scars you've earned
for simply being alive,
the heavy head,
the aching limbs,
the tired eyes, so tired
you sleep-walk
this life…

Take your dreams, the ones that
offer you no rest,
the thoughts
that offer you no way out,
the longings
that pitch tents up
in your shoulders,
the past
that leave teeth-marks
in the curve of your neck,
the voicelessness
that mutes dreams so quickly
they cannot be turned into song
and sung out into the night.

Take your battle-ready body
down to the water
and submerge.

Walk out
until the gentle tide
lifts you up
and all you have left
above the surface
is breath and heartbeat.

Feel what it is like to float -
despite the armor.

Feel each scar being freed
from the constraints of the body,
each thought forming into drops of oil,
marbling across the water -
the thick salt
rinsing dirt from open wound.

You are not your body,
nor its contents,
nor its badges and losses,
you are not the matter,
the mind, the darkness,
nor the deep, deep ache.

You are
what's left above
the tide:
the breath, the weightlessness,
the eyes lifted up toward wonder,
and the silent, drifting current below…

And although you must
return to the shore,
you carry salt's medicine
and breath's refuge
within you.

Use them both, often,
in the form of exhale and tear,
as if prescribed by the soul
and remedied by the Heart.

Cast them out, without shame,
into your earthly world.
Make protective circles
around you with them.

Make them ritual and food
for everything that
causes the body
to forget its origin.

And return to them
- *this breath and this water* -
when gravity and pain
remember their purpose,
so you can remember yours.

THE•FUTURE

If you tend

your future

relentlessly,

it will be abandoned

by the greater hand

that cares for it.

If you insist on

taming

what has an instinct

to be free,

you will wonder your life

upon the leash you gave it.

Your future

was made wild

and the only hand

you may lay upon it lies:

in the body beholden to you

here and now.

In the love you show yourself

that will hold you tomorrow.

In the nourishment you

honor yourself with today,

that will sustain you for a lifetime.

In the seeds you are sowing,

the dreams you are molding,

in the dough you are kneading,

in the beads you are threading,

in the holes you are mending…

those single actions

that cannot yet show you

a picture of its final form.

Try not to hold onto

what is yet to take shape,

what is not

solely yours

but being nurtured by

a much greater caregiver.

And know this;

that all that life

fulfills its potential -

and yours is no exception.

THE•FRIEND

She came out of the blue one day

when you were caught up in the

raging fire of hopelessness.

She spoke so gently from the smoke

of your own inferno, that you had to pull

yourself away from the room

and walk out into the fields

to chase after her words

that were being carried off

by the passing wind.

She whispered back words of hope,

and with a knowing of your future

that was so intimate,

you dared not doubt her.

She told you that you were ok.

And you felt it

in a way that

no one else has made you believe.

She told you that you were beautiful.

And you believed her

in a way that

no one else has made you feel.

She rubbed your cheek,

tears running iridescent.

She stroked your hair

and embraced you into the cleft

of her shoulder.

It felt like you had come home,

like you had finally arrived

in a place of peace.

You were shrouded in love,

blanketed in the fine silk of soft words.

You were yourself.

Just as you are

and just as you have always been.

You were lifted sweetly,

feet brushing the tips of grass,

back to the ashes of your life.

She parted

by lighting a fire in your heart,

so you would remember

that not all flames destroy.

- Self-love

THE•UNDOING

It is from the heart

that we feel the ache

of displacement

and it is through

the heart

that we redeem our sense

of belonging.

The same place that

experiences the death

is the one

we are reborn from.

So look to where it hurts -

place a palm upon

the radar

that humbles this hand

and follow it inward.

Picket a sign

above this place

that says;

"to all who pass,

there lies in this void

both

wound and remedy,

both

split and repair,

both fire and frost -

be gentle

for as I am mending

so too am I coming undone."

THE·FALCON

Through a broken tile on the roof of an old Norwegian stave church, a young falcon found its way into the humble congregation.

There sat five old women praying far apart from one another, as old wolves might stake out there own territory. These five old women praying looked up at the bird and each made a silent prayer...

One, whose feet and fingers were broken and then healed and set, said to herself,

"Pesky bird! What is this world coming to? My life seems to be filled with hopelessness and I cannot find a way to change it. Why would a bird come to this sacred place and disturb me in my troubled times? I must pray harder for my needs and despair..."

And the second old woman looked up as far as her sore neck with the creak in it would allow, and said to herself,

"Oh, I see! It's a sign that I have prayed well today, what a blessing, a visit by a holy thing, an apparition to give me the strength to see me through this dark night..."

And the third old woman said,

"What is that thing I see up there? You can't be a bird! If you really are the Holy Spirit, you better leave me a feather on my pillow as I wake, so I know you were real!"

And the fourth old woman said,

"Oh my God, I see you there. Perched upon the end of the wooden ship, strung onto the ceiling beams. Oh, my dearest Lord. Strike me with your wings so that I may bleed and that this bird may peck me into pieces so I may be carried up to heaven's nest and feed me until I am full of you. Please hear my prayer."

And the last old woman...the last old woman...saw nothing that the others saw...

For she was busy letting herself down through the broken tile in the roof of the old stave church, and she was soaring and wheeling over the heads of the old praying women... giving them something to pray for.

THE·BODY·OF·WATER

And as confident as you may feel at times seeking and striving towards what you think you need in your life – your small efforts do not touch upon the blueprint of bounty that the universe has planned for you when you surrender to it. Give yourself up to the current that ebbs and flows in the direction of truth.

To return to your flow and center is to let go of both shores, reminding yourself that you are not confined to the banks of promise and fear.

And although you are water, your body is not confined to ox-bow lakes or shallow marshes - but to the expansive ocean herself.

THE·WILDER·KNOWING

You are here, dear soul, in this unknown wilderness we call life – and you can never really lose yourself, only briefly forget that you are already found.

The path of a hand-made life snakes and saunters in ways you cannot foresee, and in that frightening place of the unknown, you will always be reminded to look deeply at where you are right now to see where the next foot is to be placed.

What keeps you lost in this life are the many distractions that lure you away from creating your own path and becoming the artisan of your own life.

It takes courage to step even one toe off the manicured road that is laid out for you – but with every act you make based in Heart, every moment of stillness before you step, every brave expansion of a comfort zone – you will gain the trust within yourself to pioneer a path of your own making.

When you feel lost and crave some kind of direction, look no further than the habits that are keeping you in a state of wandering. We often lose ourselves when we don't have time to simply *be*, we lose ourselves when we don't prioritize our creative work, and we lose ourselves deeply in the humdrum of predictable routines. These are the hungry wolves that trail you; the habits keep you trailing your own scent.

Know that the northern star is unconditionally guiding you, so too is the moss upon the tree, the moon phase, and the sun's gaze. It just takes a moment of stillness to look up, to walk slow, to breathe in wakeful presence.

Seek less direction from others, from man-made lights and wrist-watches and look inward towards your own wilder knowing.

THE·FALSE·SUN

It twists our spines and crooks our necks towards its bitter warmth, promising us that if we worship it, then it will comfort us and take our pain away.

We stand withering together under this false sun but the longer we look at it, the more we believe we need it to feel good about being so bent and misshapen.

To believe that there is something wrong with us is to believe in this false sun.

To contort ourselves into shapes that are not native to our bones is to turn away from our roots.

There is a pure and nourishing sun right here within us that asks for nothing other than to turn back towards the truth of who you are.

Heart is our Sherpa back towards inhabiting our true shape and loving ourselves again.

THE•BELONGING

No, you don't belong.

Because where you do

won't ask you to change,

won't ask you to fit in,

won't ask you to

make yourself smaller,

to be accepted.

That homesickness

for a place that you've never been.

That longing

to find peace in the presence of others.

That lingering loneliness

humming in the distance…

is not telling you

that you don't belong here

but is telling you

that you do belong somewhere else…

somewhere far beyond the ordinary.

Follow the tan smoke signals,

the smell of burning pine

and damp earth.

Follow the peaty moss,

the bent eaves,

sun's shadow,

high crescent moon,

water's reflection,

until you meet Heart;

the one who's voice

flows through your blood.

She will guide you to

home's hearthstone.

THE•QUESTION

If you were asked to - you could find a reason for being here, right now.

You could go back a few years, if not more and trace your finger through the sand to end up right here. If you were asked to - you could find meaning in what you were doing today.

You could reassure the doubt and fear with a single stroke of presence. If you were asked to - you could give the best possible explanation for why right here is a fundamental stepping stone to being where you want to be tomorrow.

If you were asked.

But you *are* being asked…every day, your life is asking, whispering, for you to trust yourself through the uncertainty and doubt - to find the meaning in what often feels like chaos.

Poise yourself over blank page and connect the dots, firm up the lines inked from tears, use heavy hand and cement your life's stony past with the belief that where you are right now matters to the greater story of your life.

THE·WISD_O_M·_O_F
·UNWANTEDNESS

We forget that there is wisdom in our shadows; that which is hidden in the umbra of our wounds.

It is in these places that we least expect to find a knowing because we spend little time simply being with our unwantedness.

However, to learn to trust the truth of our experience we must go against the grain of a society that has coalesced us into losing contact with that wisdom of the unwanted.

This is a society that has normalized consistent happiness as a yardstick for one's success.

However, happiness is neither a gauge nor a barometer for how well we have lived - and it is neither a static goal nor an end destination.

It's our darkness that breaks us open. It's our heartache that refines us into a raw material and makes beautiful shapes of us. It's our struggle that creates scars and indents upon our bodies, so we may have places for joy to pool. It's our longing that throws us into the kiln and enkindles us. It's our uncomfortable experiences that strip us down and bare our bones to the open fires of change.

The only problem with darkness is its unwantedness.

Healing is the art of realizing that happiness is not the opposite of pain - but the outcome of our loving presence being applied to *all* the parts of who we are.

THE·FALSEH<u>OO</u>D

Every hurt hides a falsehood.

A buried belief that seeded such a great lie

that no one knew of its poison,

not even you.

And every time you hurt,

you validate that belief

that perhaps

you don't deserve that happiness

or you are unworthy of real love

or real success

or real joy…

But take away that belief

and you are left with what *is* real:

That it is just a feeling,

just an expression of past

caught up in itself,

a tag.

a thorn,

a thread

that leads to nothing of beauty

or substance

or truth.

If you are written and rewritten

by the falsehoods of hurt's validation,

so can you be recreated

by the nourishing narrative

of Love's endorsement.

THE•REPLENISHED

See beauty in your unwanted, rainy days,

a gift from the gods and all

that's still glorious;

making sweet and fertile

the dry and depleted.

The damp cloth

that raises the bread.

The wet hand

that washes child's face.

The womb

that holds life...

So too do these days offer alchemy

in their devotion to replenishment

THE·CHILD

You have a fearful child within you that has taken the entire world upon her small shoulders. She stands weary in iron-cladding, too heavy to bear the burden of hurts long fallen.

Have courage to notice her innocence today, to see that her guardianship of you is born from the fierce desire for life to protect itself, and hold her lovingly within your Heart for just a moment.

This is the way we forgive our past for making soldiers of our innocence.

THE•REWILDING

Let bird's beak nestle

twig into your hair.

Let her create warm nest

that home her young

in those strands

that have spent years

under iron & dye.

Let snail leave silky trail

across those soles that

have carried you great distances

without ever having arrived

at a destination.

And let bee make honey

from your sorrows,

a little pollen gathered

from each flowering wound.

Let spindrifts wash your tired face.

Let daisies furbelow your toes

and spider web its thread

through open cuts

like stitches.

Let roots grow,

inwards,

from ever skin cell

reaching towards your center,

weaving you in from corner to corner

into heart's home.

Let butterflies

escape your lips,

one transformative spell at a time.

Let moss grow in your darkness,

granting you direction

towards liberation.

Let mind be as it is -

a vast sky of space,

allowing each cloud

right of passage.

Let yourself stand still,

long enough for

ivy to enshroud you,

willow enfold you,

and earth to hold you…

And all will be healed.

THE•REMAKING

Times of despair can be your remaking.

And when you reach that point

where you feel there's nothing left to lose…

lose yourself.

For only when you are no longer holding on

to who you think you are

and what you think you need -

will you realize that you are

still alive…

and that you can still breathe.

And that perhaps what you were

holding on to

was actually weighing you down,

and that the real death is living a life

carrying ghostly burdens…

And that real liberation

only began once you lost

everything you thought you needed

to be free.

You will be remade from these ashes.

Just remember that you too,

belong to the inferno.

THE•DREAMER

Plant many dreams.

Tend to them lightly

with a feather-like touch.

Sing to them softly

whenever spirit calls

and give them space...

fields and fields of space

to grow in their own time.

Take walks at dusk,

slowly brush your hands

over their flowering tips,

inhale their heavy scents

and spend just enough time

with them to appreciate

their beauty and potential.

Each dream holds

a variation

of life yet lived,

a story yet told,

and you do not know

which will offer you

the medicine you seek.

Your only job

is to care for the pollens

of hope that lie

within each dream

and to walk barefooted,

and open-hearted

through this landscape.

For just as nature

achieves miracles

through patience,

so too will mastery

be made of your dreams

given a little

time.

THE·EXP<u>O</u>SED·R<u>OO</u>T

Exposed roots,

they protrude through

the surface

with their twisted

and misshapen forms

shallowed,

they break the surface where

the topsoil has come away.

You too have sacred grounding systems

that call to be dug down deep

into the very core of you

so that they may hold you in those

heavy winds, those eradicating fires

and those floods of hurt.

Externalize your validation –

and your roots will bubble up, bared.

Seek to change the mirror

rather than what is being reflected –

and your soul-source

will crown upward from its

rich & peaty underworld

into a world of scarcity and famine.

Hold opinions as solid as gold

but which inhabit no worth

and your foundations will be inverted,

upturned from being

multi-faceted, dynamically supported

and self-sustaining

into a one-dimensional husk.

Keep finding

and nourishing your taproot;

the inner and vertically descending

part of you that holds,

restores and maintains

balance between both worlds.

THE·GIVER

Today, give less.

Give less of yourself

away to those who

barter for your worth.

Give less explanations

for why you are the

way you are.

Give less energy to

being validated by anyone

who's not in your skin.

Give less of your time

to those who are impatient.

Give less responsibility

to others to make you happy.

Give less heart

to those who squander it.

Give less noise

to an already deafening world.

Give less belonging

to the conformed and

hang out on the fringes.

Give less life to that

which needs to be buried.

Give less…until you are so laden with time, care, space, silence, joy, trust …that you can finally turn around, and give something back
to

you.

THE•MOUNTAIN

How do you take the mountain home?

How do you hold onto

that un-splintered version

of yourself as you traverse back into

the foothills of everyday life?

How do you return

to the smallness

and troubles

that multiply under

routine and magnification?

How do you bottle up the vastness

of perspective

or carry the expansive horizon

in the cup between shoulder blades?

How do you keep that perfection of heart

without losing it to daily blemish and fray?

How do you grasp the fullness of hope

in a palm that has so much else

to hold?

How do you let your wilder places

grow, untamed and full,

away from those hands ready

to till up soil

and make ready for rows?

How do you take the mountain home?

THE·BELOVED

To be in this moment

without asking it to change.

To see the smallness of thought

through the greatness of *being*.

To live innumerable lives

through the tenderness of one.

To take refuge in heart

when all else abandons.

To follow thumbprint inward

toward the center of true belonging.

To crease and fold life into shapes

that lure mystical creates into being.

To churn the rawness of hurt

into velvety butter through

the consistency of Heart.

To brave wilder ways

that lead to rememberings

of roots and sovereignty.

To know the slow and speak the subtle,

intimately and devotionally.

These are the ways

this life

can become our

beloved.

THE·LANDSCAPE

Stand within yourself

and open your eyes to

state of landscape you inhabit.

Look toward the windswept trees

of hurt

bent over,

their canopies

hugging the ground

in protection.

Look toward the familiar

raging rivers,

slicing through

any softness of earth.

Look at the coarse

and brittle flowers

that open so shyly

close to the earth,

never blooming

too full,

never taking up

too much space,

never occupying

itself wholly.

Look at the sunless sky,

how it withholds its warmth

and allows patches of

ice to collect over any depth

of water.

How many times

have you fallen through

to that lifeless landscape,

fed yourself on its offerings

but always felt undernourished -

acclimatized to its harshness

but always felt a vagabond?

There is another landscape

within you,

but it takes a homecoming,

a journey back to the

wildflowers and lush planes

from which you were first awakened.

Where love soaks

beds of blooming confidence.

Where winds don't misshapen

but gently fold the eaves

to meet the sunrise.

Where your crevasses

are measurements of depth

and not indicators

of faultlines -

and soft moss cushions

the soil beneath your feet,

enabling you to walk

this long journey without

losing yourself to emotional wear.

There is another landscape to be inhabited

but it begins with knowing

that it's ok

to let this one go.

THE·RECIEVER

Everything comes to you that belongs to you — but first, you must remember your capacity to receive it.

The meaning of 'to receive' is rooted in the Latin word, *Recapio* — meaning to take back, or re-gain what has been lost. To receive then, is really to reclaim something that has been forgotten or momentarily lost, and you do not need to be a certain way or attain a certain status in order to remember what is already yours.

Worthiness is inborn and traced back to the seed that first gave you life. You received life without a belief that your body was unworthy of holding it. In fact, your body knew that life belonged within it.

To receive is to remember that you are this container created with the capacity to bear an entire universe within itself.

To receive is an invitation to play with this universe again, as you once did as a child, when you heard trees whisper out spells through the eaves and when you pocketed ordinary pebbles as treasured keepsakes.

There have been years of wonder, innocence and an ability to insatiably receive, within you. Without caring how full your heart was, you once kept feeding your soul with more of what immortalized it.

Unlike what you have been taught, there is no exchange made in being able to receive - there is only alchemy.

This ability begins by remembering that the body receives the breath without believing it is unworthy of receiving life. Just as the flower receives the sunlight without shame for its need to be nourished. Just as the moon receives her luminous face without feeling it underserved because she still hides a piece of her darkness.

Receiving is attunement between something beautiful and what is most valuable within you – it is an ability to be fed something of real substance, that you are then able to offer others with the fullness of your heart.

If you are constantly at odds with yourself and your ability to receive, you will always be asking for more but never able to open your palms and hold it – never able to open the door to what is being delivered because your hands are so full of fear, doubt and unworthiness.

Holding onto false narratives clench your fists closed. These are the stories that limit the natural conversation between you and your life. And there cannot be a partnership with the universe when one side cannot receive what the other is offering.

Unworthiness is a deeply biased narrative based on the idea of an exchange. Behind the inability to receive lies the belief that you are not deserving - or that you need to bargain with your value in order to receive something - often lesser – than your worth.

But it is not an exchange – it is a reclaim of what you once knew with your whole and tender heart.

Everything comes to you that belongs to you – but first, you must remember your capacity to receive it.

What is your capacity to regain what has been momentarily lost?

THE·REAL·LOSS

Losing yourself is not the worst thing that can happen. You could find yourself further down the path looking back at this very moment, wondering why you did not take the opportunity to explore the freedom of this unanchored state.

You could look back and wonder why you did not slip through the hart-tongue ferns while no one was looking and follow the faint trail of this unknowingness deep into its underpass.

What could be worse is finding yourself where you always thought you wanted to be but it not being what you hoped for, having never stepped off the path of certainty to ramble after those crimson-winged creatures who were in fact distractions of destiny.

What is worse than losing yourself right now is finding yourself years down the track looking back at this moment and longing to tell your unfound self to disturb the gravel and descend into the under groves - the place you were meant to lose a destination in order to gain a journey.

THE•LATTICE

Do not wait

until you are empty

of pain, before you

allow yourself

to be happy.

Perhaps you

are not meant to

be completely one thing

or another

but multi-faceted,

dynamic, interwoven;

a lattice, both

healing in one direction

and simultaneously

coming undone in the other.

Allow yourself

to be both.

Both becoming

and abridge.

Not full

of one thing

but empty of all,

so you can embody

the vessel

to which

all experience

finds its

place of

belonging within.

THE•REBIRTH

Do you hear it? Across Heart's plane, through lung's valley, pooling into top of belly? A song, unknown to all - but you.

You recognize it, somehow.

You've heard it your whole life, laced in whispers, repeating your name. It speaks of moon's yearning to return to its own darkness and trickling stream's thirst to be part of ocean.

In all the ways it knows how - soul's siren calls for your return.

And return it must be. And a journey it must take. For no homecoming is ever recognized until one has ventured too far away from where they belong.

Do you remember that time you got lost as a child? Stepped off the stony path to follow the flutter of violet wings - and you fell long and deep into the tall, silver ferns. That moment when your fear turned into an inexplicable sense of freedom, a world full of adventures in the undergrowth, unseen from the road.

A taste for wild unknowingness coursed across your skin like lightning.

That was the call. Those are the moments when soul and you coalesced.

And now, where is that call? Where is that freedom? Where do you now seek for lightning skin and moonstruck awe - and in what ways does your soul's siren speak to you?

It is only in listening to this voice that will you walk this life assured of joy. For even though other roads may be easier - no other song will sound as sweet and no other journey will carry you as far.

THE•MAGICK

How can you

see the magick

when all you see is

the mediocre,

the hurt,

the struggle?

But if pain is all you see

then how can you

possibly see anything else?

Magic is not so much something

you occasionally do

behind closed doors

or in the quiet

treasures of time you

pocket for yourself...

It's a way of living your life -

a way of approaching

the world you move

through

and the relationship

you have with

everything you come

into contact with.

True magick lies in the details,

not only in the wonder of tiny heart,

plant or habitat,

but everything within yourself too -

the multifaceted aspects of your being-ness,

the Mirabella, honored by the bones of your

creativity,

the alchemy that exists in your willingness

to be with what you are yet to know

and your understanding that

what you do not know

may be the greatest

wisdom

of all.

It begins with you, dear one,

with the magic that

is not made

from

but

of

you.

THE•NATURE•WITHIN

The sun dapples the floor ahead in light and and shadow. Tell me friend, do you notice how it takes more than just light to create this masterpiece upon the floor? So too do shadows and light play a part in the beauty of who you are.

Let's walk into that clearing where branches part…

Can you see how the flowers grow where space is given? So too are you able to grow, given a little room to breathe, to be yourself, to bloom in your own time.

Notice the moss on that thick trunk? Can you see your pain in that moss? Can you see how it grows in the darkness, away from warmth and light – what you might consider an imperfection to the beauty of that tree, is fundamental in understanding direction. The moss soaks up the shadows making them into substance; north, it grows, giving you a healing compass to follow.

See here, how easy it is to dig out old weeds, brambles and pull at ivy in the dead of winter when nature's bones are bared, when there is no energy left to fight the season. You can see what is what, what needs to go and what goodness there is left in the soil.

So too do the winters of your life offer you opportunity to take stock of what needs to change. Little attention is given to improvement when life is in bloom and lush with joy. Take heart that these times are just another season and one worth baring yourself to.

See how the debris from last year's fall have collected beneath each plant to form the nutrients that help it thrive? So too is your old self a foundation for who you have become today, nourishing where you now stand with the shellings of who you once were.

There is no shame from what soil you blossom from – dark and peaty substances make for the most vibrant blooms.

THE·VISION

It doesn't matter

what you see before you.

What matters

is what you see within yourself,

and how you bring

that into the world.

Offer the bounty of your heart

to the scarcity of these conditions,

the fullness of your lungs

into cavities of hopelessness...

Leave roots and seeds

in the homes and hearts

of those who have long

suffered from

the famine of kindness.

See, from the inside out,

this life

not as it is,

but as it could be,

given your tenderness.

THE•TRANSMISSION

Just as you wail loneliness through the chords of your heart, so can you tighten these strings to communicate with others.

Sit with your ache and give it sound, grieve it, unbound by the confinements of shame.

Let loneliness sing itself through the silence until it becomes a meeting place for all other homeless hearts. Soon you will see that the company you seek is seeking you; an empty heart sits by an abandoned radio wave listening for your signals of hope.

Let love and its longings connect you to these singing strings being strummed throughout the world.

For loneliness is not at all silent, but a deafening transmission being heard by all of our hearts.

THE·BAREF_OO_T

All this time,

you've been searching

for the right shoes

to navigate this

unforgiving road...

When perhaps

all you needed

was to find a path

that you could walk,

barefooted.

THE·TRUER·LOVE

It is easy to fall in love with the idea of your future self because she is yet-tangible and full of promise & potential. You apply what many call 'self-love' to her; this refined and perfected version of yourself, making it easier to accept her for who she is because she is on the path towards betterment.

But all true love stories begin in the dark, in the trenches and aqueducts of who you once were.

Between the one who is immortalized through memory and the one who's warm breath can condense upon mirrors.

True love stories begin when you trace your fingertips over the scars and thank them for reminding you that you are still here.

Love each ripple & every 'V' shaped trail that pans out behind you. Not because you know you will one day change...but because you already have.

THE·INVERTI<u>O</u>N

The well of your sadness

holds too,

the quantity

of your hope.

The reservoir of your pain

holds too,

the span

of your awakened heart.

The emptiness of your longing

holds too,

the substance

of your home.

Whatever creates pits and hollows,

chasms and ravines,

in you

are not at all

gauges of your lack…

but truer dimensions

of your capacities.

THE•POTTER

Let life shape you.

Surrender to the

hand that curves you,

to the nicks and notches

that are given not

in carelessness but

in passion for your existence.

Feel the places within

you that are thick with

hurt's debris and know

that it is just more material

to use in your making.

Surrender to Heart and see

what she will make of you.

THE•QUIET•PLACE

Walk the fields

where the

feather and maiden

grass grows -

and find the

small patch of earth

that has been

packed and pressed

heavy by deer's body.

Lie your earthly body down

against the warm ground,

and curl your knees up

against beating heart.

Let the weft and warp of you

be spun by earth's

curved and flexing loom.

Let starry cradle

hold your darkness,

turning tears

into constellations

that light the midnight sky.

Be still and rest,

return to the nest of all beginnings

and endings,

let nature seep, sow,

heal and

grow

you

from a place of quiet cede.

THE·W<u>O</u>LF·AND·THE·ARR<u>O</u>W

For the one who hurt themselves

Every day, you wake to the wolf and the arrow. Both are lethal. But one is of your own making.

The wolf curls up by your feet at night and slumbers until the early hours. Upon waking, her heavy paws pad down upon your chest. She reminds you of her ominous presence as soon as your eyelids part. Oh, the burden to wake up every day with a wolf at your heels!

And throughout your day, you stumble over her, avoiding those artic eyes that hold so unnervingly upon your fragile form. And as you lay your head down to rest, her wet snout breathes heavily into the curve of your neck. Her whiskers softly prick your throat, her weight, seemingly impossible to shift.

The wolf is your emotional pain. She is the weight upon your heart. The knowing eyes that follow you throughout the day. The sometimes-reassuring comfort. The howl you hear in the middle of the night that comes from your soul, longing to belong to something greater. And then there is the arrow. It is made by your own hands. You created it in defense against the wolf. How else can you protect yourself against such a fatal creature?

But every time you grip an arrow in your hand and throw your shoulder back to aim for her soft and vulnerable belly, you pierce an exposed piece of yourself. Every time you can't bear her presence, you cast an arrow in vain towards her, like an old woman casting her shoe at the cat who weaves her legs into knots.

But, like a boomerang, this arrow finds its way back towards you. Perhaps its feathers are skew, bent in crescent shapes? All the hours you've spent crafting this arrow, to always land up wounding yourself!

And so it goes. The wolf and the arrow. Both create so much pain. But one is natural. The other is hand-made. One is a fundamental part of life. The other, a misguided form of self-protection.

This is life as we all experience it. The wolf; a fundamental part of life who embodies the inevitable challenges and difficulties we all face. We can call her our painful longing to be part of something wilder. She is a part of us. Her grey hair, a very deep shade of wisdom that can only come from a certain type of pain.

But, the arrow. That hurts us much more than wolf ever could. Our arrows are self-constructed tools of protection. It's our way of hurting ourselves so something else can't. It's our ego. It's our false narrative. It's everything we close our eyes, ears, mouth and hearts to. It's our need to be seen and heard, no matter the cost. It's our hurtful habits. It's our need to be validated by something other than ourselves. It's our righteousness and our ignorance. It's our cover. It's our bent arrow.

We have the chance, however, to disarm ourselves and be with what is here; open, vulnerable, accepting to what is at our heels.

We have a chance to make friends with the wolf in our life. There is no need to pet it. No need to be in conversation with her or find comfort in her presence - but acknowledging her is imperative towards any form of self-healing.

When we say good morning to her and perhaps even throw her a sideways wink when her most devious nature comes out to play, we become very empowered.

She is then no longer *an unwanted part of us*, but a natural part of life and something we can perhaps even learn from if we were to spend a little time getting to know her.

Our pain is truly an invitation to walk beside a rather mystical creature who can show us the way home.

We often believe that we are able to protect ourselves from what is most unwanted. But perhaps it is more the fact it is *unwanted* that hurts us most...

How is your arrow serving you right now?

Have you invited your wolf to tea yet?

THE•REMEDY

It's not real friendship just because you're lonely. It's not real freedom just because your cage is refurbished. It's not real healing just because you can't feel it anymore. It's not real bravery just because there's an absence of fear in that moment. And you haven't gained real love in the loss of yourself.

In order to know what is true and most sacred in life, you must know yourself first. Otherwise every search will lead you to another substitute, another placebo, another watered down experience that leaves you with an insatiable thirst.

Know yourself. You are the remedy.

THE•WILD, DEAR•CHILD

Go into the wild dear child

and unpack before you go,

the lessons you've been taught

about the dangers and those fearful beasts

that lie in the unknown.

Go into the wild dear child,

take little of what brings you ease.

Be brave and trust Heart,

for she's the keeper

of wisdom

that lie far beyond these trees.

Go into the wild dear child,

and remember the

unmapped path is the one

that leads you home.

Follow moonlit clearings,

and unlearn your fearings,

unlearn your voicelessness,

your othering,

your hopelessness

and the inheritance in which

old wounds were sowed.

Go into the wild dear child,

and know this before you go;

that the fear you fear is not out there…

but within you alone.

THE·HOPE

Look at how beautiful you are, dear soul, as you walk these dark woods, making friends with the raven and the full-bellied moon, untangling your bones from the bramble, unbraiding fine threads of spider's web from your hair.

Look at how beautiful you are, dear soul, holding fiercely onto that small flame of hope, caged between two palms, held tight across chest, you brave a storm that has no concern for your survival.

Look at how beautiful you are, dear soul, walking onward as wind gathers you up under its downy wing. Why you don't just allow yourself to abandon that flame, I do not know. How easy it would be douse it with pools of rain, open hands, and be rid of its responsibility.

But still you push onward, thorn scars, bark scrapes, howling darkness as companions, you hold on - you hold on to that hope.

Look at how beautiful you are, dear soul, how vulnerable, how soft your fragile form weaves these woods, how you hold onto and protect that piece of you that lights but an inch of the way ahead.

How beautiful you are, dear soul, for waking, for rising and for walking onwards - despite it all.

THE·SOVEREIGNTY

Dear soul,

keeper of time and space,

guardian of the precious people,

whose soiled palms

pull at your hems.

I know you feel the world's burden

is yours to bear -

but it is not so.

It is up to you, however,

to take it upon your own heart

to heal your own Self.

So weave

your two worlds;

make flush your two skins

and become united

with what never was disembodied.

And before you cry to the hills

and send for the medicine makers,

know this:

Rituals are not prescriptions

for the sacred

but small expressions of divinity

that already reside

within you.

And wisdom is not

held by secret-keepers

but in the knowing of

your own bones.

And words are medicinal;

inoculations for

nocturnal minds,

small doses of strength

made every day to combat

the spread of separateness.

And you are not a healer

but an alchemist,

transmuting the pain of laceration

into sacred wholeness.

Go now,

make sovereignty of quiet.

And tend to the magick

that is not here for you

but of your making.

THE·END

There is really nothing left to do now, except affirm your allegiance to the inner knowing that seeded this change. To remember the longing that initiated it in the first place. To continue clearing the obstacles that obscures your next becoming. And to count, even by millimeters, the increase of your joy and wellbeing.

As you finally emerge with greater ownership of your values and gifts, remember to honour the as yet fragile nature of new life.

Tell yourself the story, again and again, of the love you offer, and the love you deserve, while your vision gains strength at the root.

And when others praise your sudden arrival, I will remember the long bravery that made your ascent.

≈

Dear honored reader,

Here we are at the end of this journey.

I'd like to thank you for reading this little book and offer you a virtual campfire on my newsletter where I would love to get to know you and your story. Who are you, where have you come from and what is your soul-sickness? After all, no story is fully healed until it has been shared.

Please feel free to stay in touch beyond my books via:

www.sezkristiansen.com

hello@sezkristiansen.com

If you felt this book would be of help to others, please **review it on Amazon or Goodreads** so that it may be seen by other wayfarers like yourself.

From my heart to yours,

Sez

≈

Printed in Great Britain
by Amazon